HOTELS
IN GERMANY

HOTELS
IN GERMANY

Magnus Trauenstein

PAGE ONE

HOTELS IN GERMANY
Copyright © Verlagshaus Braun, Berlin.

First published by:
Verlagshaus Braun, Berlin
www.verlagshaus-braun.de

Published in 2004 by:
Page One Publishing Private Limited
20 Kaki Bukit View
Kaki Bukit Techpark II
Singapore 415956
Tel: (65) 6742-2088
Fax: (65) 6744-2088
enquiries@pageonegroup.com
www.pageonegroup.com

Distributed by:
Page One Publishing Private Limited
20 Kaki Bukit View
Kaki Bukit Techpark II
Singapore 415956
Tel: (65) 6742-2088
Fax: (65) 6744-2088

First edition 2004

Editorial staff: Per von Groote
Editorial office: Franziska Nauck
Translation: allround Fremdsprachen GmbH von der Lühe
Graphic Design: Michaela Prinz

ISBN: 981-245-213-3

Printed and bound in China

2004 2005 2006 2007 2008 / 10 9 8 7 6 5 4 3 2 1

Contents

Foreword

The reservations have been made. Above the wing of the plane or near the emergency exit, smoker or non-smoker, first class or second class, stalls or a private box, a table for two, not too close to the band. The holidaymaker knows his stretch of beach, the family man his traffic jams, the businessman the self-service check-in machines. Travel takes many forms and all lose their novelty soon enough. And in the meantime each traveller's individuality must submit to the vacuum-packaging and reduced leg-room of the drive for uniformity.

Decisions, decisions. Will it be one night or two? Will a wake-up call be necessary or, like a lovesick writer, will the guest languish in bed until the sun sets for the night? Does he want the familiarity of being called by his name, or does the frequent stayer still prefer the anonymity of a first-timer? Is Madam happy finding the lift by herself or would she like her luggage carried? Are guests at ease opening up the minibar? Are they completely without inhibition when letting a used towel slip to the floor? Do others think of entrusting valuables to the hotel safe, or are they travelling with an absolute minimum of baggage – or none at all?

The luxury associated with preoccupations such as these is no longer the preserve of the few. Gone are the times when crossing a border was a major undertaking. In an earlier age the word 'travel' had a quite different ring to it: more than anything travel was equated with time lapse, and there was pleasure in its passing, and no hastening after deadlines. This epoch of ocean-going liners and the Hamburg-America Line marked the birth of the modern travelling class.

The advent of the modern age brought a levelling-out of class distinction. Consumption was within the means of everyone, mobility was a sign of progress and belief in the worthiness of travel seemed inseparable from the idea of success. These brave new maxims inflated the value of something generally held to be worth striving for: status.

Perhaps out of an urge to reject their own satiety, perhaps as an acknowledgement that nothing is off-limits to their imagination, and certainly as a direct response to the needs of modern travellers, a higher class of hotel service has emerged that is not limited to offering excellent service and state-of-the-art equipment. Distinction like this no longer distinguishes; it is already the standard. Nowadays it is a quite different range of qualities that attract the modern traveller.

So: the reservations have been made. One does not emerge from plane or train to surrender the decision of one's night accommodation to the whims and wiles of a taxi driver. Friends recommend this hotel or that; one has heard of such and such a hotel and is keen to test it out for oneself; and one is just as likely to return to a place which has already proven itself. The idea of coming and going as one pleases, of availing oneself easily and lightly of the comforts pertaining to a guest – or of declining them without one's self-assurance being taken for granted… this is luxury.

A hotel is no longer simply a place of rest, no longer just a matter of temporary rights exercised over a room. A hotel makes a connection between public and private spheres. The narrow line separating the alien from the familiar has become a connecting door between the two, as reflected in the hotel's concept and its architecture. The image of the modern business traveller as nomad of the modern age is adopted by many hotel concepts and rejected by others, for every person crossing the threshold of a hotel is as alien as he or she is des-

tined to be alien: reception – that haven of security –, the friendly staff, the helpful, unassuming personnel... The hotel defines its guests as protagonists in a parallel reality. Just as if they had awoken from a reverie, our travellers, emerging from the fug and sensory welter of dreams, are able deliberately to call up a similar world that echoes the one they have just experienced.

This applies to famous establishments as much as to modern hotels, whose architecture and interior design are breaking with convention. In the classic, traditional hotel concept, lovingly cherished, guests are typically welcomed and coddled like VIPs. Never too forward or assuming too much, yet always at pains to second-guess their every wish. The rituals of these luxury hotels, relics from a bygone age, oozing world famous historical presence from every pore, satisfy the needs of their demanding guests, be they tourists, artists or politicians, without seeming to exert themselves and without ever coming into conflict with the modern world. This unique hotel culture is its own unmistakeable hallmark – and it is a trump card that is always held, however often it is played.

The other side of the coin is represented by a new generation of hotels that has used unusual design and some extraordinary concepts to become a major feature on the hotel landscape. Each hotel is unique in form and character and the related elements of their modern styles are so diverse as to defy categorisation. The hotel, functioning as stage, establishes the broad parameters and the scenery changes within these. The skilful blend of diverse architectural elements and lighting creates truly liveable rooms and a lively mix of tensions. Guests are simultaneously onlookevs and protagonists. They can choose their roles and are in the enviable position of

being continually exposed to the tangibly unique charm of architectural artistry.

The sheer diversity of the German hotel landscape is impressive. Classical forms rub shoulders with modern lines. Naturally both can never be allowed to compete with each other, and neither of the forms would wish to. Each seduces in its own way.

A third trend is also discernible. A hybrid form of hotel architecture blurs the distinction between the two genres, preserving the historical infrastructure while, at the same time, integrating modern components. Buildings are put to different uses and the history associated with them determines the architecture of their interiors.

Architecture's process of imitation and innovation produces modern hostelries whose builders are at once pioneers and mediators between two worlds. Their feel for form, materials and spatial relationships dovetails agreeably with the progressive developments within a hotel culture boasting an unparalleled repertoire of bold gestures and idiosyncratic ambiences.

And what of that passion for travel, currently absent, that was mentioned earlier? No one can claim to be completely free of constraints. All those about to set off on a journey, unless they are on holiday, are apt to lose sight of the essence of journeying as they busy over the motive for their travels. Yet if they light on accommodation whose form manages to block out the petty preoccupations of their everyday lives they will be in a position to feel truly at ease. These are hotels whose physical boundaries are never visible, since time and space appear to follow their own, distinct rhythm. Guests have been welcomed into a reality which they, alone, could not have created for themselves.

Magnus Trauenstein

Architect
Carl Stöhr
Interior Designers
amj Design |
Anna Maria Jagdfeld

The Dorint Sofitel Quellenhof Aachen combines the respective traditions of the neo-classicist Grand Hotel, designed by Carl Stöhr in 1913, and the imperial baths in the Royal Spa. Thanks to sensitive renovation of the elegant architecture and the far-eastern culture that influenced the fitting out of the rooms, the hotel underwent a non-invasive transformation and was imbued with an ambience of timelessness. The natural materials used and the judicious décor confer on the hotel an impression of absolute tranquillity. The sensation of warmth and security is crea-

ted by such features as American walnut panelling, floor segments of finest teak and couches upholstered in Kravet suede. Granite and Verde Maritaca stone from Brazil in many of the spa areas embody the peace associated with steadfastness and hone one's appreciation of the essence of architecture. Far-eastern accessories and stone replicas provide visitors with an omnipresent and stylish backdrop.

QUELLENHOF AACHEN
DORINT SOFITEL

DAMPFBAD

Interior Designers
Büro Ezra Attia,
London (1997)
Living Design,
Stockholm
amj-Design |
Anna Maria Jagdfeld
(2004)

The legendary Adlon by the Brandenburg Gate was reopened in 1997. The luxury of superlatives that Lorenz Adlon created back in 1907 was destroyed in a huge fire in 1945. Reconstructed on the original site and rounded off in 2004 with an extension offering new rooms and luxury suites, the hotel seduces with its blend of elegance, opulence and the sophistication of modern technology. Gold leaf wallpaper on the ceilings and full length French windows in the suites testify to a lavish approach to décor, while cherry and myrtle wood furniture, gold-coloured fabrics and soft, mock-suede cushions add a timeless touch of elegance. Anna Maria Jagdfeld's classical modern interior design fits perfectly with the overall concept of the hotel. The finest of fabrics from exclusive manufacturers in Germany and Italy promise guests the highest standards of comfort.

Hotel Adlon
Kempinski

BERLIN

Architect
Helge Sypereck
Interior Designer
Beate Weller

Like all other art'otels this hotel is dedicated to world famous artists – in this case two: Andy Warhol and his photographer Christopher Makos. The rooms of the hotel contain a total of 150 Warhol originals and 180 works by Christopher Makos on the theme of "Travel and Guests". The building on a street corner gives the impression of being higher than normal, surrounded as it is by structures of varying heights and the staggered angles of adjacent streets and building rows. The Cotta sandstone façade, seen from a distance, appears as a fine sculpture featuring

windows set flush to the wall and columns two floors high marking the main entrance and restaurant. The artist's works are integral to the atmosphere of the interior and the hotel's public areas set up a constant interchange with art. The rooms are extraordinarily colourful and filled with the presence of the artist, creating an impact as soon as the guest enters the room and switches on the light.

Architects
Nalbach+Nalbach
Interior Designer
Hon. Prof.
Johanna Nalbach

The former parcelled structure of the listed Ermeler building resonates subtly in three visual realms, each distinct in materials and structure. The baroque building incorporating rococo elements has been carefully restored, new architectural and design components added. The result is a controlled clash of Minimalism and baroque unity. The overlapping of interior with exterior and the dovetailing of new and old are an integral part of the architects' plan. The opposite bank of the river is visible from the two-storey hall, on a line of sight across the historic glass inner yard and through the building's glass entrance. The rooms are dominated by the interplay of rudiments of minimalist thought, the atmospheric power of light and the warmth of four different types of wood, allowing materials, form and colours to develop their own aesthetic and fulfil their primary function of providing each guest with a short-term haven of privacy in characterful surroundings.

Architect
Werner Weitz
Interior Designers
Herbert Jakob Weinand
Cornelia Müller

This hotel is located in the Bleibtreustrasse, a quiet side-street intersecting with the Kurfürstendamm in the central 'west city' district. With its avant-garde design, its classical elegance, its historical infrastructure and the pleasing colours and materials, this 19th century, middle class townhouse offers a complementary mix of modern and traditional. The distinct styles of the individual floors provide an example of this: the pale yellow rooms on the fourth floor are set against the stark black and white graphics on the fifth. On the lower levels

it is a shimmering blue that predominates and gives the inner open-air area and the Blue Bar a character all their own. The untreated oaken furnishings, handles of semi-precious stone – all were designed exclusively for the "Bleibtreu". All the materials used were chosen for their natural, environmentally friendly qualities.

BLEIBTREU

BERLIN

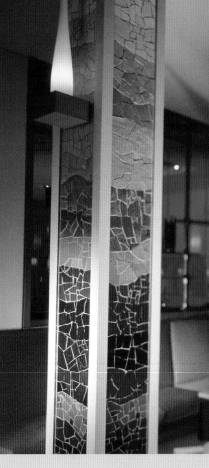

Architects
Plan GmbH |
Dipl.-Ing. Peter Becker
Interior Designers
k/h Büro für
Innenarchitektur und
Design | Harald Klein,
Bert Haller

The Dorint Sofitel on Gendarmenmarkt square, with its view onto the French and German Churches, occupies a corner building that served as Party training headquarters in GDR times and is now listed. The original character of the building is only visible in the foyer area, whereupon it gives way to contemporary interior architecture. The rooms giving onto the square vary in size but many have small balconies and feature brick-coloured velour and cognac-tinted bedside lights. Traditionally precious materials such as stone and smoked glass are juxtaposed with state-of-the-art textiles. The function room and conference area, also used in the GDR era as an event hall, has been given a one-colour-fits-all refurbishment to "conserve" its original socialist décor. A glass floor illuminated from below provides a stage for new (transparent) political functions.

AM GENDARMENMARKT BERLIN
DORINT SOFITEL

Architect
José Rafael Moneo
Interior Designers
zed AG | Hannes Wettstein

A wall of reddish sandstone rises serenely upwards into the Berlin sky. Immediately apparent is the Grand Hyatt's class, not overdone but rather the product of high-quality materials and meticulous care at the construction stage. The result is a clear, unadorned line – modern yet timeless. An example is the lobby with its cedar panelling. The eye is drawn to the chandelier-shaped light at the top and the alabaster-fronted box lighting. The rooms, with their furniture of light and dark stained cherry wood, seduce guests with their uncluttered character.

Bauhaus photographs underscore the spareness of the design. Blueish grey marble is a feature in the lavish bathrooms and a perfect accompaniment for the black marble of the washstand. Dual access by sliding door from the hall area and the drawing room allows daylight to penetrate the bathrooms – making a stay here a doubly pleasant experience.

RELAXATION
AREA

Architects
BHPS Architekten |
Johannes Heinrich
Interior Designers
k/h Büro für
Innenarchitektur und
Design | Harald Klein,
Bert Haller

From its prominent position on Budapester Strasse the Intercontinental, with a chequered façade listed as worthy of conservation, has long been a feature on the landscape of Berlin's West-City. The latest phase of renovation and expansion, including the newly-built south wing and its lively arcade on the ground floor, has given a new sheen to the hotel that is now a bridge between the old centre in the west of the city and the eastern part of the metropolis. The building impresses with its white, granite front and the matching aluminium window fittings. This

business and conference hotel combines modern interior design techniques with stylish exclusivity. The rooms, redesigned from scratch, reveal a new and extravagant concept behind the room design. High-grade woods and stone exude objectivity. Sliding doors and cubes that can revolve on their axis challenge spatial structures. A club floor, with its own access, offers seclusion and individual wish-fulfilment.

Architects
kessler+kessler
Kadel Quick Scheib
Interior Designers
Vogt + Weizenegger
Lemongras

Situated on the famous luxury shopping street, the Ku'Damm 101 is a study in minimalist design. Deliberate elimination of all but the essentials has created an inviting atmosphere free from excessive glamour. The rooms, reception, lobby and bar have all been created along the lines of modern interior design. The idiosyncratic yet opulent setting makes for an up-beat ambience that is set to relax and inspire guests. The colour scheme is a nod to the architect Le Corbusier: with deep, restrained shades and light colours complementing each other

naturally the resulting harmony comes across as cheerful and beneficial. First class materials such as rubber flooring, exclusive furniture from young German designers and snugly stylish bathroom design are additional factors contributing to the overall luxury of the establishment.

WELLBEING AT THE KU' DAMM 101

Architects
wwa architekten und
partner |
wolfram wöhr
gerold heugenhauser
Interior Designer
Flum Design

The thinking behind the Madison was influenced by its location amid the high-rise buildings of the city centre. The building is frequented by the public and yet on the upper floors there is privacy for the guest. The mix and colour of materials used in the hotel's façade includes terracotta and wood – consciously chosen for their ability to age attractively. The character of the building's exterior transfers well to the cosmopolitan atmosphere inside. Spacious rooms and suites are testimony to a contemporary design concept. Their friendly colour scheme and unimposing

furniture create a hand-crafted style all its own. The relaxed atmosphere extends to the new, recently-designed lobby, the Qiu Lounge on the first floor and the wellness area with its breathtaking views from the 11th floor, all places where guests can linger in a cultivated environment unseparated from the throb of modern life.

Architect
Bernd Albers
Interior Designers
Neumayer & Partner

At the architectural heart of this 5-star hotel is a 35-metre high air well surrounded by columns and host to a 30-metre high wall sculpture with close to 28,000 light-emitting diodes. This spectacular light installation, designed specially for the Marriott, creates the illusion of a golden yellow stream cascading steadily down the wall. With the colour of its up-and-down façade of bright limestone the building exudes a warmth and class harmoniously conveyed also in the yellow painted rooms and suites. The guest accommodation also features mahogany furniture and materials and fabrics in vividly coloured floral patterns. The Marriott chain has chosen a historical location for its first hotel presence in Berlin. On the same spot where the Hotel Bellevue was built 115 years ago the Berlin Marriott now stands, completed in January 2004 in the Beisheim Center at Potsdamer Platz.

Architects
PB Sagir
Interior Designers
GRAFT Berlin –
Los Angeles

Completed in March 2004, the flowing lines of the Hotel Q! are instantly welcoming to the traveller. The foyer with its warm lighting is at once a point of arrival and rendezvous. Linoleum cladding is a unifying feature of ceiling, walls and floor. Even a weightless, floating astronaut could rest his head here, far from the standardized sleeping quarters offered by Corporate Identity hotel chains. The interior designers have created futuristic, multi-functional rooms. Where a diagonal wall can serve simultaneously as spatial delineator and furniture the canons of classical architec-
ture are thrown to the winds. Individual elements undergo a blurring and multiplication of function. In the rooms and suites individual areas likewise lose their functional specificity. Here, too, the topographical approach to work surfaces confers dual functions on many areas. The architecure's landscape theme is roundes off in the body-temperature warmth of the sand room in the wellness area.

Architects
nps tchoban voss
Interior Designers
BHPS Architekten |
Johannes Heinrich
Virgile & Stone
Mahmoudieh Design

This luxury hotel opened in May 2004, its most striking feature being the ultra-modern AquaDom. This large, cylindrical aquarium is the main architectural attraction of the area. Hotel guests can experience the hotel's third dimension using a special lift, yet the AquaDom is not the only element showing off the hotel's pleasantly transparent character: there is the reception made of glass and the subtle use of illuminations which gradually change colour and are carried forward into the colours and materials of the "Aqua Lounge". The deep red tones of the restaurant and the hues of its wooden materials make for a warm and cosy atmosphere. In the modern conference areas, each with its individual colour scheme, cherry wood and lighting arrangements that vary according to the time of day and the occasion both create a welcoming yet neutral environment. The contemporary elegance of rectilinear design is also apparent in the guestrooms and suites.

Architects
Hilmer Sattler Albrecht
Interior Designers
Hotel Interior Design
(HID) | Peter Silling

The Ritz Carlton, Berlin fitted out in a style that harks back to the late Empire era, is the final large-scale project on the Potsdamer Platz precinct and rounds off the eventful history of this centre of urban development in Berlin. The construction material, largely visible, is a bright, beige-coloured limestone from Portugal that gives the building a lightness despite the deep furrows of its façade and the bronze windows. The classical interior boasts the tradition of a Grand Hotel. Marble flooring, chandeliers and Stucco Lustro on the walls complement each other perfectly, making for an unique atmosphere. The dimensions of the foyer area lend everything an extra degree of size and luxury. The furnishings in the rooms and above all in the suites testify to high standards in both construction and comfort provision. The fine cherry wood furnishings were specially manufactured in Italy for the hotel. Numerous antique items are on display here and can be admired as in bygone days.

THE RITZ-CARLTON®
BERLIN

Interior Designer
Karl Lagerfeld

This splendid mansion was built in 1912, commissioned by Dr. Walter von Pannwitz, the Kaiser's personal lawyer. The residential rooms and art collection reflected one and the same period – the 18th century – and the hotel's imposing hall, with its luxurious and prestigious furnishings and sweeping lions staircase, was pure Renaissance. The comprehensive restoration and re-design of the entire interior was undertaken by Karl Lagerfeld, with meticulous attention to detail. The result is a very special, luxury hotel in the swish residential area of Grunewald in Berlin. The impressive lobby and lounge and the bar and fireplace all radiate elegant charm and exclusivity. Rooms and suites, all with marble baths, are individually and tastefully decorated. In a style reminiscent of classical Rome, the spa area on the ground floor looks out over the 3000 square metre of parkland that surrounds the hotel.

SCHLOSSHOTEL
im Grunewald

Architects
BHPS Architekten |
Johannes Heinrich
Interior Designer
Cornelia
Markus-Diedenhofen

Much of the old Schweizerhof Hotel was demolished and entirely rebuilt. A single original section on Burggrafenstrasse survived, although it too was completely redesigned on the outside and within and was connected to the new building on Budapester Strasse via the basement. Yellow sandstone covers the façade of the new 9-floor building, interspersed with square window areas coloured in anthracite. The main entrance and the lobby with its lifts rise in a conglomeration of glass verticals. Luxurious ostentation on the inside has given way to the purist elegance favoured today, a style that resists the temptation to be fashionable. The comfort, transparency and generosity clearly discernible in the interior design concept is enhanced by the hotel's well-defined lines, the warmth of its colours and the use of woods and stone. One example of this is the repetition of the façade's sandstone in the interior décor of the lifts. The thought-provoking paintings of Ter Hell hang throughout the hotel.

SCHWEIZERHOF BERLIN
DORINT SOFITEL

Architects
gmp . von Gerkan, Marg
und Partner |
Meinhard von Gerkan
Partner:
Klaus Staratzke,
Nikolaus Goetze

The Swissôtel Berlin in the Ku'damm-Eck occupies a new corner building on the Kurfürstendamm. Guests enter a foyer three floors high before ascending to reception in two glass lifts. A glass roof to the inner courtyard above provides pleasingly bright illumination. The Grande Gallery functions as fulcrum between the foyer and restaurant of this 5-Star hotel. Expanses of glass in both rooms provide stunning views of the Kurfürstendamm. Three panoramic lifts whisk guests to the rooms and junior suites on the upper floors and the two executive floors at the top.

Light-coloured wood dominates in all rooms. A low sideboard connects the wide windows with bed, chair and other fixtures, combining horizontal continuity with the warmth of light wood.

swissôtel BERLIN

AM KURFÜRSTENDAMM

A Raffles INTERNATIONAL HOTEL

Interior Designer
Harald Schreiber

A cool façade of glass belies the hotel's name. Softness and smoothness are apparent only on entering. Warm materials are prominent in an interior that still retains a clarity of form and a contemporary aura. Colours continuously change and blend on the ceiling of the foyer. The Tauerngrün stone of the floor extends as far as reception and into the cosy inner courtyard. From their geometric beginnings the shapes become more abstract and eventually peter out in the sand, creating a link to nature. The adventurous concept of the rooms has the bath separated from the living quarters not by walls but by a delicate partition. This openness is continued in the smooth, ceiling-high windows. The dark red leather of the bed's headboard contrasts with the dark brown wood of the writing table. The comfort of the surroundings is rounded off by the deep red of the carpet.

HOTEL VELVET

BERLIN-MITTE

Interior Designers
Neumayer & Partner

In the heart of the Black Forest, surrounded by nature, sits the Schlosshotel Bühlerhöhe. Far removed from the hustle and bustle of daily life the Schlosshotel seeks to provide top-rate service in a romantic and luxurious setting, something it achieves confidently and artlessly through its exclusive comforts and atmosphere. The shades of baroque in its interior design, with warm browns contrasting with the lighter beige and sandy colours, result in a non-invasive opulence which cuts an ideal balance between quality and quantity. Individually designed

guestrooms offer views of the surrounding woodland whilst a number of drawing rooms, each with its own décor, provide the venues for all manner of encounters. Following extensive renovation the hotel today is a playground of leisure pursuits and wellness activities – modern facilities that complement the more traditional accommodation and catering areas, without detracting from the establishment's romantic aura.

Interior Designers
Lang-Ladenbau GmbH

The Lennhof stands for the combination of tradition and modernity. The impressive half-timbered building – the architectural core of the hotel complex – forms part of the old built-up area on the fringe of Dortmund and is surrounded by expanses of greenery that give the area a countryside feel. Another rustic feature is the romantic terrace with its grape-vine pergola. Spare, contemporary design provides a more modern touch inside the hotel, where clarity of aesthetics is supplemented by meticulous attention to detail – resulting in simplicity without coldness.

The listed building from the 14th century, with its 10 single rooms, 23 double rooms and 4 modest suites, is one of the city's smaller, more atmospheric hotels. Its two conference rooms equipped with state-of-the-art technology meet the needs of a wide range of events and offer their organizers the dual advantages of a bucolic setting and an urban environment with a well-developed infrastructure.

hotellennhof

Architects
AIC – Architekten
Ingenieure Consult |
Gerd Ruepp
Interior Designers
"Living Design"

Built at the height of the Baroque period, the reconstructed Taschenbergpalais has housed this Kempinski Hotel since 1995. Whilst from the outside the building recalls the époque in which it was constructed, its stairwell having been rebuilt in accordance with its listed status, the interior design is modern and luxurious. A certain severity to the contemporary lines creates a deliberate contrast to the baroque whole. The high-quality furniture is eye-catching, with its red elmwood and the royal blue fabric. The elegant rooms and suites are high,

measuring up to 4.8 metres from floor to ceiling. The baths too are roomy, with black, polished granite and specially angled tiles used in their construction. The Kronprinzensuite is a luxurious highlight of the hotel, boasting items and features brought in from all corners of Europe. The upholstered furniture harks back to the baroque in form and colour, as do the assorted lights and lamps.

Kempinski
Hotel Taschenbergpalais

DRESDEN

Architects
Thomas Lau,
Mark-Hendrik Blieffert
Interior Designers
3meta | Evi Märklstetter,
Armin Fischer

This Hamburg hotel opened in 2003 in a former 1950s office building. The thinking behind the establishment revolved around transformability of room function, so that the use to which a room is put can be altered at a moment's notice. This strategy, coupled with a dynamic lighting system, allows the creation of new spatial environments and ambiences. In the course of a day, for instance, the adjustable mirrored wall "bathes" the lobby in a variety of illumination moods. Rooms destined for group use are permanently fitted out for the hosting of get-togethers.

Not only hotel guests are welcomed in this way: invitations are extended to many outside visitors, who are encouraged to sample the hotel's gastronomy and participate in events. Guest rooms borrow from the 1960s and '70s in their style of décor, the choice of furnishings favouring simple lines and functional niceties. Light blue and aquamarine pastels and brilliant white confer a buoyant atmosphere on the rooms.

Architects
Planungsgruppe IFB
Dr. Braschel GmbH
Interior Designers
k/h Büro für Design und
Innenarchitektur |
Harald Klein, Bert Haller

The interior design vision toys with proportion and opposition just as it juggles contrast and harmony. So it is, for example, that one side of the valuable, brightly-coloured marble abuts the smooth stone floor, which in turn is host to a number of high-pile carpets. In a distant section of the lobby is a clearly defined archipelago of sofas, accentuated by oversized, silk lanterns. Reception and hotel bar, judiciously placed cubes, are recognizable as such. Transparent walls in the bar create a VIP lounge with amorphous couches, comfortable chairs and a sideboard with built-in screens. Metallic coloured wall cladding in the bar sits alongside Emalit glass and precious walnut wood, all bathed in red, futuristic light. The external lift shaft sits majestically behind reception. The rooms and suites continue the material impression and colours established in the public area. Warm greys are juxtaposed to brilliant white, the purest of felts to darkest marble.

AM ALTEN WALL HAMBURG
DORINT SOFITEL

Architect
Klaus Peter Lange
Interior Designers
Regine Schwethelm,
Sybille von Heyden

After 10 months of construction in the listed coal depot of a former gasworks in the Bahrenfeld district of Hamburg the Gastwerk opened in 2000. An idiosyncratic 'loft hotel', bright and airy, has sprung up here offering a compelling symbiosis of industrial romance and modern design. The original brick walls, the old windows and the infrastructure have all been preserved. The tall windows in the striking entrance hall bring light pouring in, giving the building a transparent feel. Despite its dimensions the loft atmosphere makes for a relaxed, homely ambience. The decision to reject luxury and trendiness in favour of simplicity and good taste extended also to the interior décor. Clarity and objectivity blend with ancient artefacts displayed at carefully considered junctures. The larger-than-life-sized warrior statue at the entrance is just one example of the unorthodox interior design, which combines tension with a sense of well-being.

Gastwerk
HOTEL HAMBURG

Architects
BHPS Architekten |
Johannes Heinrich
Interior Designers
Robinson Conn
Partnership Design
Consultants |
Richard Morton

The interior design of the Inter-Continental Hotel Hamburg was extensively refurbished in 1990 and 2001. The style shift from traditional to contemporary considerably lightened the character of the hotel. Light woods and glass were now used for the furniture and a refined choice of colours were now favoured for curtains and fabrics. A side-effect of this was that relatively small rooms now appeared larger. A number of pairs of rooms were also made into single, larger suites, and cherry wood furniture was added. Bathrooms were designed to open directly into the room, adding an element of tension to the overall layout. A new, open kitchen was built in the ground floor restaurant. Curtains and furniture here were selected for the extent to which their contemporary design perpetuate the garden theme. Fine dining is available in the "Windows" Restaurant, whose traditional cigar lounge and seafaring echoes are a throwback to an international style of décor.

Interior Designers
Partner Ship Design
concept
Sea Cloud Suite)
Architekten Hertwig,
Meyer-Stromfeldt
realization
Sea Cloud Suite)

The snow white gabled front of the Kempinski Hotel Atlantic Hamburg has brought it the alias "White Palace on the Alster". One of Hamburg's top addresses, it offers spacious rooms designed to a restrained pitch of luxury. A comprehensive programme of renovation began in January 2002 and is set to create 195 completely refurnished rooms and suites. The BMW Suite is especially remarkable, combining existing top-notch architecture, including high, stuccoed ceilings, with first class materials, light and design borrowed directly from the world of luxury cars. The incorporation of BMW's familiar colours rounds off the effect. The hotel's 95th birthday will also see the unveiling of another interior decorating high point: the Sea Cloud Suite. This suite mirrors the maritime character of the cabins of the barques Sea Cloud I and II. Yellow and red woods and darker wood tones are used here to create an atmosphere of warmth.

Kempinski
Hotel Atlantic

HAMBURG

Architects
Kleffel, Köhnholdt
und Partner
Interior Designer
Pierre Yves Rochon,
Yvonne Golds –
Real Studios Limited

Le Royal Méridien Hamburg has taken its concept from Art+Tech-Design: here contemporary art – 600 original works by Hamburg artists are on display here – meets state-of-the-art technology in an intimate encounter set against an aesthetic background of neutral, transparent materials, the idea being to use as few materials as possible: light-coloured maple wood, steel and glass. Furnishings are spare, surfaces have been kept transparent, showing off the clear, shimmering colours of the painted panelling to their best effect. The key element in the rooms is the glass

engravings on the beds' headboards that were designed specially for the hotel and complement the artistic statement. Technology here is more than telecommunications: it is above all lighting techniques. Art requires excellent equipment if it is to be presented in its best light.

Interior Designers
Raffles Holding

This most traditional of Hamburg's hotels lies in the heart of the city, on the banks of the Binnenalster. Despite the many changes it has undergone the building bought by the restaurateur Friedrich Haerlin in 1897 still appears seamlessly pristine. The interior design is no less elegant, exuding an ambience of timeless luxury. Precious antiquities in the rooms create a culture of spacious exclusivity rounded off by comfortable areas of seating. The Haerlin gourmet restaurant, with its antique Chippendale and Art Deco furniture and the 500-year-old Gobelins from

Flanders, provides one of the hotel's aesthetic highlights. In 1995 an old section of polished Caucasian nut wood panelling was uncovered behind the walls of the Jahreszeiten Grill. Using old photographs as a reference the entire restaurant was then restored in the original Art Déco style, thus providing visitors with a trip back in time to a long-forgotten age.

Raffles Hotel Vier Jahreszeiten
HAMBURG

Architects
Jan Störmer Architekten
Interior Designer
Matteo Thun
Lighting Designer
Robert Wilson

The Side Hotel is located close to the Hamburg State Opera and the city's business district. The hotel comprises two interlocking sections, the front part addressing the height of the surrounding buildings, with a double façade of glass that acts both as a noise insulator and temperature regulator. The rear section, decked in greenstone cladding, is 12 floors tall, two levels being devoted to suites embracing the front section of glass. With its austere approach to materials the Side Hotel is emphatically minimalist in its interior design. In all areas of the hotel contrast is the guiding principle in the design of surfaces, whether it be rough stone juxtaposed with glass or dark, treated Sucupira wood alongside glossy white surfaces. Atmospheric lighting plays an important part in emphasizing certain shades and hues. Harmony on the one hand and abrupt breaks with style on the other create a tension in the integral unit that is the "Side".

Interior Designers:
Atelier Centrale,
gemeinnützige GmbH
"Arbeit und Lernen
Hamburg"

YoHo-Hamburg, the young hotel is a refurbished house dating back to the post-Bismarck era. Built as a training project, the hotel is an example of a new way of combining private initiative and public sector social involvement, providing a place of integration for different cultures, age groups and social classes. This has been reflected in the design, with a compromise being achieved between old architecture and more youthful features, between oriental and European styles. Built in 1904, the building has been totally renewed on the inside and provided with a new lift and stairwell. Clarity and modernity have informed the design of the new construction, conferring an autonomy on the building while maintaining a balance between old and new. The hotel is simple in form yet fine and elegant in character. The identity of items within the hotel comes not from their surface appearance but from their sheer material quality. This approach has imbued the hotel with its clear and calm atmosphere.

Architects
HPP Hentrich-Petschnigg
& Partner
Robert A. M. Stern
Interior Designers
amj Design |
Anna Maria Jagdfeld

The "White Town at the Seaside" is the oldest – and until the '30s was the most exclusive – seaside resort in Germany. The Kempinski Grand Hotel Heiligendamm has been nurturing this tradition since 2003. The Grand Hotel and five other buildings are a throwback to the location's classicist past. Contemporary design techniques have exploited the traditional style elements to create an interior of understated luxury that is the antithesis of pomp and museum-like splendour. The décor of the place skilfully reflects the physical setting and the history of the location: subtle stripes that recall the hues of the Baltic, materials and carpets in beach colours, sofas and chairs that reproduce the shades of meadows, clouds, dunes and beech woods… the rooms are decked in nature's gentle tints. Traditional craft and authentic materials are the twin pillars of olden-day architecture and latter-day extensions alike. And each building has an atmosphere all its own.

Kempinski
Grand Hotel

HEILIGENDAMM

Architects
nps tchoban voss
Interior Designer
Alison Brooks

On Helgoland, Germany's island far from the main-land, flanked by sand dunes and red cliffs, lies the Hotel Atoll. The hotel was founded in 1999 with the aim of providing an experience that combined aesthetics, the natural world and comfort. This vision is reflected in an interior that incorporates elements of atoll topology into a unique design. Colours from the south seas, shapes reminiscent of waves, an illumination scheme that recalls the upper, sun-flooded fathoms of the ocean… The theme begins in the foyer with quirky elements such as the curved walls

of copper, a floor-level porthole with a view of the pool and a bar in the shape of a futuristic, novelly-lit mussel. The unconventional layout in the rooms creates an exciting atmosphere: a wall unit made of jet fighter fibreglass, a multi-use design feature, that combines the functions of chaise longue, table, mini-bar and wardrobe in a single piece of furniture.

atoll helgoland

Architect:
Schweger & Partner
Interior Designer
Cornelia Markus-
Diedenhofen

The Dorint Novotel Karlsruhe Kongress was designed to a large extent with the requirements of a modern hotel catering to business and conference guests in mind. The bright building is not only excellently fitted out: it is also directly linked to the congress centre by an elegant, 12-metre long glass bridge. The interior design includes a remarkable lighting arrangement that first strikes the visitor from an illumination unit hanging above the reception counter. A steel staircase of sculptured quality is designed to clash with the symmetry of the entrance hall. The hotel's greys and browns, coupled with the natural materials of the surfaces, create a pleasant atmosphere suggestive of business and commerce. The interior architects also achieved an admirable combination of acoustics, robustness and design quality in the materials they used.

Interior Design
Thomas und Gudrun
Höreth

The "Alte Mühle" Hotel ranks both in its architecture and its cuisine as an exclusive establishment. The restoration of the 800-year-old mill lasted 4 years. Twelve separate buildings centre on an inner court-yard and a romantic garden. Alterations to the yards, the guest rooms and the vaulted cellars set great store on preserving the Middle Ages flavour. In numerous instances old materials from demolished buildings were used. The venerable façade and a variety of antique features both inside and out con-jure up an old-world ambience not to be found elsewhere along the Mosel river. The rustic character of the ensemble as a whole, as determined by the overall vision guiding its renovation, is also reflected in the design of the rooms without the effect being overdone. Lightweight materials, bright colours and those little details that enhance the specificity of each room all go towards creating a noble yet home-ly atmosphere.

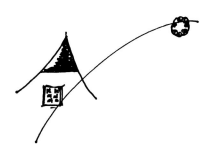

Architects
Architekten HKR |
Rolf Kursawe
Interior Designers
Architekten HKR |
Rolf Kursawe

In the spring of 1997 the Hopper Hotel et cetera opened its doors within the walls of the old Cologne monastery of the Merciful Brothers of Montabauer. The establishment dispenses with the superfluous details common to many other hotel concepts and favours a classical, modernist style without adhering to any particular fashion. The idea behind the furnishings is to make the monastery's cells seem larger than they are. The two-floor chapel destroyed in the war now houses an independent restaurant. A wall-sized oil painting recreates the chapel's apse,

destroyed in the war. The spare austerity of the architectural vision is also reflected in the materials used. Steel, glass, wood and exposed concrete dominate. The result testifies to sensitive handling of the existing, historical infrastructure, a furnishing concept that is modern yet timeless and non-invasive and a contemporary approach to the selection of paintings for the interior.

Architects
Architekten HKR |
Rolf Kursawe
Interior Designers
Architekten HKR |
Rolf Kursawe

In 1999, after an extended period of refurbishing, the Hopper Hotel St. Antonius opened in the former journeymen's building of the Kolping Society, five short minutes from the cathedral. The name of this particular Hopper hotel is taken from a hospice set up in 1904 on the site and dedicated to Saint Antonius. The rooms and suites have adopted the ethos of the former hostel and extended it into a modern hotel concept. As in the case of the first Hopper hotel 'et cetera', the wood and steel and the white paint of the Kambala parquet floor are all remi-niscent of the early journeymen's quarters. Wash stones in the baths recall the original purpose of the building. Existing, historical infrastructure has been preserved and set against contemporary architecture and design. The restored staircase gable, the original vaults in the former refectory, Mettlach floortiles and numerous other original materials all underpin the unique character of this hotel.

HOPPER
Hotel St. Antonius

Architect
John Seifert
Interior Design:
k/h Büro für
Innenarchitektur und
Design | Harald Klein,
Bert Haller

With its "light and shadow" design concept the Cologne Intercontinental uses lighting both to produce a creative work atmosphere in communications environments and to bring about evolving shadow effects in certain areas. Large, low suspension lamps in the lobby mark the location of groups of chairs. A large spiral staircase situated within a translucent lantern of fabric links lobby with first floor. Focussed lighting also features in the restaurant "Maulbeers" in the form of oversized lights and a mirrored wall that reflects images ad infinitum. The Kaminzimmer, or Fireplace Room, with its stucco ceiling and ancient 16th century fireplace, provide a counterpoint to the new interior architecture. Floor-to-ceiling mirrors in the rooms convey the impression of space, the painted bedsteads a sense of cosy security. An elliptical writing table that turns on its axis is both a work surface and a vantage point from which to admire Cologne and its cathedral.

INTERCONTINENTAL®
KÖLN

Architects
Guder & Hoffend
Architekten
Interior Designers
Guder & Hoffend
Architekten
Lighting Designer
Christian Türmer

The unusual thing about the Hotel Santo in Cologne is its lighting architecture, the idea of there being a link between illumination and emotion, which has given it elevated status among the hotels of the city. Illumination is the key element in a concept that recognizes the subjectivity involved in appreciating ones surroundings. Kreon lamps provide a constantly changing play of light. Coloured spotlights or lights directed from unexpected angles, for instance from the corners or from the floor itself, give the impression of space and time fusing as one entity. This new way of perceiving things is made possible by the genteel, avant-garde atmosphere, itself a product of the extravagant furnishings in the rooms and bathrooms. Materials appear to flow into one another, an example being the juxtaposition of Jurassic sandstone in the floors and top-quality oak wood. This multicoloured oasis of light asserts itself as a novel living environment that provides visitors with unfamiliar sensations while at the same time giving them a feeling of calmness and strength.

santo

Architects
Architektenpartnerschaft
Dipl.-Ing. E. Grimbacher
Interior Designers:
k/h Büro für
Innenarchitektur und
Design | Harald Klein,
Bert Haller

To choose this hotel is to step onto a stage whose scenery is constantly changing. The floor of the playfully designed lobby of the Radisson SAS Köln is a pattern of squares interspersed with stripes. Chairs, sofas and Ottomans by Minotti and Frigerio have been positioned as if at random. The reception gives the impression of being an elongated sculpture of wood and stone. The smooth, gleaming counter of varnished jacaranda is in direct and stimulating contrast to the rough surface of the counter's base, a weathered plinth of Jura limestone. This is a design concept repeated throughout the hotel. Similarly widespread in a variety of forms is the plate glass, especially prominent in the guestroom. Its satin coated surface provides a soft, slightly blurred reflection of colours and materials. Reflected light gets trapped in the dark red velvet drapes and headboard of the bed, there to remain in suspended illumination.

Interior Design:
Johannes Adams

Many features of the 4-star The New Yorker Hotel conjure up the cult neighbourhoods of Manhattan – Soho, Chelsea or TriBeCa. Surrounded by architecture that harks back to the industrial history of the area, visitors can enjoy an oasis of calm in an eccentric environment, yet without having to make do with visual boredom. The New Yorker offers modernity and comforts in equal measure, nothing repeats itself and everything is slightly off-beat. Not long after opening in 1999 the design hotel, with its 40 rooms and three junior suites spread over four floors, had become recognized as the place to be for cosmopolitan creatives. The burgundy-coloured velvet chairs in the lobby, the dark blue lights in the guestrooms, the furniture and lamps were specially made for the hotel by owner-architect Johannes Adams. The idyllic garden with its 40m^2 pond of goldfish provides a peaceful space for rumination which also spills over into the hotel's interior through the large glass frontage.

THE NEW YORKER HOTEL

Architect
Max Dudler Architekt |
Thomas Kröger
Interior Designer
Max Dudler Architekt |
Thomas Kröger

"Dispense with the superfluous" runs the design credo of this hotel. A flamboyant, one-off work of architecture, it juggles boldly with form, materials and orthodox perceptions. The building's exterior, a monolithic sculpture of light grey Portuguese granite, gives a foretaste of the sober finery waiting to be experienced. Minimalism meets elegant purism: no wallpaper, no curtains, no ornamental cushions, no unnecessary knick-knacks. In their place: pure, white walls, black floors overlaid with slabs of asphalt, unadorned but carefully selected furnishings. This policy is repeated in the rooms: light grey and white predominate with colour provided by Black Monday designer furniture and a crimson shade that filters the sun's rays. Not only the design but the clarity of layout imbue the QUARTIER 65 with a non-invasive, family atmosphere.

QUARTIER 65
HOTEL

Interior Designer
Kevin Voigt

With the opening of the Advokat towards the end of the Nineties Munich received its first designer hotel and one which clearly delighted in flamboyant details associated with its time. A successful blend of art and design places busts, paintings and flower arrangements throughout the hotel, an effect that is topped off with carefully selected furniture and sensitive illuminations. The Sixties look in the lobby includes cherry wood wall panelling to the level of the door gables, easy armchairs, travertin cube tables and a stone floor. The rooms exude a warmth with their

earthy shades. They are lightly furnished, with the accent placed on details such as the glowing apple on whitest of white cushions. The rooftop terrace, with its unusual Eternit furniture, offers a glimpse into typical Munich courtyards. This pleasant oasis is concealed behind the hotel's unremarkable '60s exterior, the breakfast room alone being on show to passers-by on the street.

274

Interior Designer
Albert Weinzierl

Extensive renovation of the former Adler has produced the Cortiina, an exclusive hotel whose clear and functional architecture sits well amidst the historical landmarks that are the Hofbräuhaus, Marienplatz and the Viktualienmarkt. As unobtrusive in character as the sandy, plaster façade are the materials, employed in the interior design, for instance oak wood taken from the area around Munich, for the panelling and roughly hewn Jurassic stone from the Ingolstadt region for the exterior of the lounge fireplace. The resulting unforced elegance is underscored with linen and leather and individual items of furniture. The open-plan rooms with their clear lines also boast a glass wall extending to a bathroom featuring sanded-down Jurassic stone flooring, polished stainless steel basins and Vola fittings.

Interior Designers
Bachhuber-Ambiente

Following extensive redesign the famous Kempinski Hotel Vier Jahreszeiten, located on Munich's swish Maximilian Strasse, has managed to strike the right balance between the traditional and the modern. Since 1858 the hotel has been associated with class and style. One has only to think of the listed Nymphenburger Room with its unique, hand-painted tiles and its porcelain art works – the perfect backdrop for exclusive events. The renovation preserved historical character while adding touches of modernity. Designer pieces from France and Italy, hand craf-

ted doors, drapes and furniture were all incorporated into the new interior. 170 rooms and suites of rooms were designed from scratch. In the function rooms, too, contemporary styles sit side by side with traditional design. A classical wall of panelling, for instance, conceals a fully equipped multimedia screening facility.

Interior Designer
Pierre-Yves Rochon

In the centre of Munich, a short distance from the key attractions and the finest shopping areas, is to be found Le Méridien München, where French flair combines with a European stylishness. Gleaming black granite lines the entrance, lead-coloured granite cloaks the columns that surround the hotel. The lobby is classical in feel, its black marble inlaid with reddish brown marquetry. In contrast, the doors to the spacious rooms and suites are of light coloured wood, which also features prominently in the bathrooms, together with brown marble. The leopard

pattern carpets, a warm mix of yellows, ochre and brick, allow guests to pad silently across the floor. State-of-the-art technology and atmospheric elegance complement each other perfectly in the conference areas, lending a particular sheen to meetings, presentations and ballroom events.

Interior Designer:
Dipl.-Ing.
Rainer Maria Kresing

The most noticeable element in modifications to the green glassed Mauritzhof Hotel concerned the new layout of the entrance area, which now extends from the centre of the building to the hotel's north side and links up with the new driveway approach. An ultramodern, 4.2-metre-high, glass drawer structure has been constructed, partially invading the attractive, severe, brick Mauritzhof edifice. The drawer ushers guests into the lobby and bar area, illuminated in pastel yellow, tomato red and bottle green. In clement weather the bright and spacious lobby opens out onto the terrace and promenade, providing a fluid transition between interior and exterior: entrance area, bar and lounge become quasi public spaces, which conveys hospitality and openness. The rooms, each with its unique layout, have adopted an international style of décor – simple lines, large floor-to-ceiling windows, high-quality materials and classy designer furniture.

Architects
Nalbach+Nalbach
Interior Designer
Hon. Prof.
Johanna Nalbach

A charming lake 15 km from Wismar provides the setting for this country hotel which opened in 1993 after careful restoration. 80 guests can be accommodated in this 100-year-old clinker farmhouse and thatched, half-timbered barn from the 19th century. Each room and bathroom is using unique materials and colour schemes. Cupboards and beds have been designed specifically for the hotel and selected items of furniture hark back to the era of the original builder. The rural beauty of the location and the Cistercian monastery (kloster) that gave the place its name both influenced the process that has created the cosy atmosphere of this refuge. Daytime atmosphere simulations are projected onto a screen in the thermal baths. The 12-metre high barn, a hall with terracotta floor tiles from French monasteries, is just one of the rooms suited to hosting the many cultural events put on at the Seehotel.

SEEHOTEL
LANDTHERME
KUNSTSCHEUNE
RESTAURANT

Architects
Jo Stahr Architekten
Interior Designers
Planungsbüro Johann
Thurner

The new building constructed for the Seehotel Über-fahrt in 2001 was conceived as an optimistic stimulant to the imagination. The result is a modern, elegant hotel that extends a friendly welcome to its visitors. The arrangement of space and light has achieved an aggregate result of nuanced subtlety, one in keeping with the hotel's exclusive design and fine selection of accessories. One principle applied throughout is the primacy of the aesthetic over mere function, of sensibility over utility. So it is that space is approached from the viewpoint of personality and

character. Recourse to this strategy is everywhere apparent and is noticeable in the design of the accommodation, for example, where each room and suite has its own individual character. This generosity of line and material value is also evident in the high-quality materials used – marble, hand-polished glass, dark woods and pure silk. The wellness area is particularly opulent, with a glass domed swimming pool and its own bar.

SEEHOTEL ÜBERFAHRT TEGERNSEE
DORINT SOFITEL

Architects
wwa architekten und
partner | wolfram wöhr,
gerold heugenhauser
Interior Designers:
wwa architekten und
partner | wolfram wöhr,
gerold heugenhauser

The Bad Waldsee golfing hotel was built on a former farm and fits well into its countryside setting, its architecture a plausible mix of old and new. The link to nature was a key element in the design. The slanting ends of the building extend into the surrounding landscape, giving the complex a striking appearance when seen from afar. The hotel's aspect is lightened by expanses of glass, unimpeded lines of sight and breaks in the building's profile. The façade incorporates a screen of exposed concrete into which the balconies, the floor-to-ceiling glass fronts and the wooden moulds of the baths have been let. The interior opens out onto a bright foyer that leads directly into the old part of the hotel: the shell of the old barn remains, with its doors now of glass, resulting in a pleasantly high yet cosy room. The guestrooms, with their outer walls of glass, have balconies opening onto greenery. Natural materials and a warm range of colours underscore the hotel's homely character.

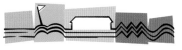

GOLF & VITALPARK BAD WALDSEE

Architects
Peter Schmidt Studios,
Tombusch & Brumann
Interieur Design GmbH
Interior Designers
Zaeske + Maul
Architekten

The Hotel Nassauer Hof is one of Europe's few truly luxurious hotels. The Wilhelminian style of the building as a whole contrasts perfectly with the classical timelessness of the interior, a convincing blend of modern times with yesteryear. The elegant hotel lounge, the reception area and the bar have been designed in warm, friendly tones and this cosy, homely atmosphere has been topped off with discreetly positioned, luxury accessories. The idea of an interplay between calm on the one hand and accompaniment on the other is continued in the rooms,

suites, the "Orangerie" and the "ENTE" Restaurants. The hotel possesses a variety of conference rooms, each with its own individual character to suit the function being staged: rooms borrow, for instance, from the styles of artists such as Picasso, Klee and Chagall. The interior architecture culminates in the swimming pool, with its own thermal spring and view over the rooves of Wiesbaden.

Architects
Henn Architekten
Interior Designer
Andrée Putman

The Ritz Carlton Wolfsburg, with its concave ring shape, bids its visitors a hearty welcome as they draw up and promises them protection and seclusion on the inside, where the warm tones of the stone inner façade embrace a Japanese garden. The classical design of the lower ground level, the three standard floors and the top floor is alleviated by a façade set forward or back according to storey. In the rooms and corridors of the elegant interior the walls, panelling and storage cupboards are of bright Canadian mountain rowan wood, with a grain that catches the eye. The discerning guest will appreciate the evident high quality of the fabrics and materials used, with their shades of cream and grey and absence of brown. The rooms' homely yet individual character is achieved with non-intrusive accessories and original works of art that are scarcely reminiscent of hotel accommodation.

THE RITZ-CARLTON®
WOLFSBURG

Johannes J. Adams
BAU-ART IMMO Management GmbH

Deutz-Mülheimer Straße 204
51063 Köln
Fon +49.221.47 33-0
Fax +49.221.47 33-100
JA@thenewyorker.de
www.thenewyorker.de

Johannes J. Adams (b. 1962) studied Architecture in Dortmund and Cologne. Meanwhile he was working in Monte Carlo, Cologne, London and San Francisco. Between 1995 and 1996 he planned and realized multi family houses in Cologne and modified the Graf Zeppelin summer residence near Berlin. From 1998 to 1999 he designed and realised the construction of the New Yorker Hotel, which he runs.

Bernd Albers
Prof. Dipl. Ing. Architekt – BDA

Segitzdamm 2
10969 Berlin
Fon +49.30.615 91 51
Fax +49.30.615 92 48
mail@berdalbers-berlin.de
www.berndalbers.com

Bernd Albers (b. 1957) worked freelance in the office of Prof. Hans Kollhoff, Berlin, from 1984 to 1987. In 1993, after a stint teaching at the ETH, Zurich, he founded his own architects office. He has also been working since 1996 as development surveyor for inner city planning and has held a professorship in design and construction in Potsdam since 1999.

amj-design
Anna Maria Jagdfeld

Friedrichstraße 71
10117 Berlin
Fon +49.30.20 94 62 40
Fax +49.30.20 94 60 10

Anna Maria Jagdfeld (b.1954) has been providing consultancy services in project development and design since 1990. As owner and CEO of "amj holding" since 1997 and of "amj design" Berlin since 1998, Anna Maria Jagdfeld has designed not only the rooms of numerous hotels but also the interior of the Japanese Embassy, the China Club and the Adlon Palais (all in Berlin).

Atelier Centrale

Ottenser Hauptstraße 39 a
22765 Hamburg
Fon +49.40.39 10 96-6
Fax +49.40.39 10 96-77
info@atelier-centrale.de
www.atelier-centrale.de

Bettina Hermann (b. 1968), a qualified designer, and Dirk Danielsen (b. 1963), a qualified designer and organ builder, founded "atelier centrale" in 2000. Bettina Hermann left the firm in January 2004 to take up a managerial post in the furniture industry. atelier centrale designs buildings, rooms, products and textiles for prestigious clients.

Bachhuber ambiente GmbH

Dorfstraße 20
84378 Dietersburg I Peterskirchen
Fon +49.8565.96 10-0
Fax +49 8565.96 10-70
ambiente@bachhuber.de
www.bachhuber.de

Bachhuber ambiente GmbH specialises in the furnishing and fitting out of hotels and catering establishments, ships and other major installations. The company sets great store on meeting clients' specific needs in order that "visions become reality and architect, client and guests can all get a real thrill from the end product." CAD technology is used in the development of each project.

BHPS Architekten
Bassenge, Heinrich, Puhan-Schulz
Gesellschaft von Architekten mbH
Fasanenstraße 71
10719 Berlin
Fon +49.30.88 71 41-0
Fax +49.30.88 71 41-66
mail@bhps-architekten.de
www.bhps-architekten.de

The architects Jan C. Bassenge (b. 1938), Johannes Heinrich (b. 1943) and Kay Puhan-Schulz (b. 1938) have been working as a team since 1976. They are concerned with planning and interior design in all its aspects. They are particularly interested in using contemporary forms of expression in reconciling a building's architecture with its specific environment.

Alison Brooks Architects

35 Britannia Row
London N1 8QH
Fon +44.20.77 04 88-08
Fax +44.20.77 04 84-09
info@abaspace.com

Alison Brooks set up her office in London in 1996 and won numerous awards for her work in the fields of municipal architecture and residence construction and the areas of interior and landscape design. Trademark features are her sensibility towards the physical surroundings and her incorporation of local art. At the European Hotel Design and Development Awards 2000 her office won first prize in two separate categories for the Atoll Hotel.

Max Dudler Architekt

Oranienplatz 4
10999 Berlin
Fon +49.30.61 51 07-3
Fax +49.30.61 45 07-1
info@maxdudler.de
www.maxdudler.de

Max Dudler (b. 1949) worked at O. M. Ungers from 1981 to 1986. Since 1992 he has run his own offices in Berlin and Zurich. Crowning achievements so far are the Foreign Office building and the Federal Ministry for Transport, which won him his first award in 1996. Following his new IBM Headquarters and the Hagenholzstrasse tower block complex in Zurich he is now preparing larger Swiss projects.

**gmp Architekten
von Gerkan, Marg und Partner**

Elbchaussee 139
22763 Hamburg
Fon +49.40.88 151-0
Fax +49.40.88 151-177
Hamburg-E@gmp-architekten.de
www.gmp-architekten.de

Meinhard von Gerkan (*1935), Volkwin Marg (*1936) and their partners founded the gmp architecture offices in 1965. Their wide range of realised concepts reaches from detached houses, hotels, museums, theatres and concert halls, office buildings, commercial centres and hospitals to transport buildings and research and education facilities. Above all, gmp has won international renown with its airport architecture and many town planning projects.

**Yvonne Golds
Real Studios Limited**

64 Great Suffolk Street
London SE1 0BL
Fon +44.20.79 28 22 11
Fax +44.20.79 28 77 11
Email@realstudios.co.uk
www.realstudios.co.uk

Yvonne Golds worked on numerous international projects including the interior design of the Royal Academy of Music, the First Residence of Cairo and Yeldersley Hall and prize winning exhibitions like "Waterford Treasures" and "In Flanders Fields". She endeavours to find unique solutions to the specific needs of each individual client.

GRAFT Berlin · Los Angeles

Borsigstraße 33
10115 Berlin
Fon +49.30.24 04 79 85
Fax +49.30.24 04 79 87
berlin@graftlab.com
www.graftlab.com

GRAFT was founded in 1999 by Lars Krückeberg (*1967) and Wolfram Putz (*1968) in Los Angeles. They were joined by Thomas Willemeit (*1968) in 2001. The office for architecture, town planning, exhibition design and music opened a branch in Berlin that same year. Along with the realisation of various projects, GRAFT is interested in overcoming the barriers between the different disciplines so as to achieve a greater creative potential.

Guder Hoffend Architekten

Köpenicker Straße 48/49
10179 Berlin
Fon +49.30.27 59 20 06
Fax + 49.30.27 59 20 08
berlin@guder-hoffend.de
www.guder-hoffend.de

Stephan Guder (b. 1964) and Matthias Hoffend (b. 1966), both architects and engineers, founded the Guder Hoffend Architekten cooperative in 1999. Both studied architecture under Prof. Conradi at the Technical College of Aachen and worked in a number of architecture and engineering offices.

**Prof. Gunter Henn
Henn Architekten**

Augustenstraße 54
80333 München
Fon +49.89.52357-131
Fax +49.89.52357-152
info@henn.com
www.henn.com

Gunter Henn (b. 1947), Professor at the Technical University of Dresden and visiting Professor at MIT, studied architecture and civil engineering. In 1979 he founded Henn Architekten, which has specialised in buildings devoted to research and teaching, production and development, administration and corporate architecture, e. g. the Wolfsburg Autostadt, the Glass Manufactury in Dresden and the Beijing International Automotive Expo.

**Hotel Interior Design (HID)
Peter Silling**

Hansaring 88
50670 Köln
Fon +49.221.17 94 40
Fax +49.221.17 94 41 00
p.s.design@t-online.de
www.hotelinteriordesign.de

Hotel Interior Design (HID) was formed in 1995 as an offshoot of IHF, itself founded in 1990. Both companies were set up by Peter Silling. Shortly after the establishment of operations in Germany the first foreign branch was set up in New York. Silling now oversees projects worldwide that are involved development, conception, construction management, interior architecture and design for hotels and restaurants.

**Hilmer & Sattler und Albrecht
Gesellschaft von Architekten mbH**

Sophienstraße 33A
10178 Berlin
Fon +49.30.284 95 40
Fax +49.30.280 71 33
info@h-s-a.de
www.h-s-a.de

The intention of the three architects is not to produce startlingly new designs but to do the best they can in drawing buildings and city out of their fixed context. They have notched up three decades of projects noted for their proportion, diversity and detail. Accomplishments range from the residential building for Jürgen Habermas and the residential block periphery construction in the centre of Karlsruhe to the planning project for the area around Berlin's Potsdamer Platz.

**HKR Architekten
Norbert Hentges | Rolf Kursawe |
Petra Rehberg Thiedecke**

Krummer Büchel 1A
50676 Köln
Fon +49.221.92 16 46-0
Fax +49.221.92 16 46-25
architekten.h-k-r@t-online.de
www.architekten-hkr.de

Norbert Hentges (b. 1955), Rolf Kursawe (b. 1956) and Petra Rehberg Thiedecke (b. 1959) founded the HKR office in 1989. Their area of activity embraces single and multi family houses, hotels and commercial buildings. They are particularly committed to the modification and refurbishment of listed buildings. Project activity ranges from 2D surveys to photo-realistic representations of future buildings.

**HPP Hentrich-Petschnigg &
Partner KG**

Heinrich-Heine-Allee 37
40213 Düsseldorf
Fon +49.211.83 84-0
Fax +49.211.83 84-144
info@hpp.com
www.hpp.com

*The express aim of HPP is to deliver high-
quality work on time and within budget,
thereby complying with clients' wishes
and expectations in matters of aesthetics,
functionality and economic efficiency.
HPP's holistic approach facilitates a sensibility towards all aspects of design from
the planning phase onwards, an awareness that also takes account of environ-
mental preoccupations.*

Kadel Quick Scheib

Behaimstraße 25
10585 Berlin
Fon +49.30.34 15 04-0
Fax +49.30.34 23 51-5
architekten.k-q-s@t-online.de

*Christoph Kadel (b. 1960), Max Quick (b.
1962) and Angelika Scheib (b. 1965) established their practice in 1993. Their work
focuses on hotel planning, refurbishing,
and construction designed for use by the
handicapped and the elderly. Their credo
involves taking design seriously and pay-
ing meticulous attention to quality. Their
success is based on consistent adherence
to these objectives.*

**Kessler+Kessler
Franziska und Daniel Kessler
creative consultants**
Freiestrasse 17
CH-8032 Zürich
Fon +41.1.2 51 86-80
Fax +41.1.2 51 86-82
kk@kesslerundkessler.ch
www.kesslerundkessler.ch

*Kessler+Kessler advise companies and pri-
vate clients on interior décor, design, corporate architecture and communication.
Their declared objective is to develop
public and private spaces into visually
communicative areas combining form
with functionality, trends with tradition.
This has led them to design communication and design concepts for hotels, the
catering trade, residential buildings and
international exhibitions, among other
venues.*

**k/h
Büro für Innenarchitektur und Design
Harald Klein | Bert Haller**
An der Eickesmühle 30
41238 Mönchengladbach
Fon +49.2166.94 63-0
Fax +49.2166.94 63-22
design@klein-haller.de
www.klein-haller.de

*The designer Harald Klein (*1953) and
the interior designer Bert Haller (*1956)
have been working together since 1998
under the name k/h. Their projects tend
to focus on gastronomy and hotels. Along
with the creation of interior design concepts, they also develop business ideas
and corporate design, budget proposals
and light and furnishing plans.*

Dipl.-Ing. Rainer Maria Kresing

Lingenerstraße 12
48155 Münster
Fon +49.251.98 778-0
Fax +49.251.98 778-10
info@kresing.de
www.kresing.de

*Rainer M. Kresing (b. 1952) studied archi-
tecture in Delft, Munich and Aachen, where
he received his degree. In 1976 he worked
in the office of Einar Thorstein Ausgerson in
Reykjavik. From 1980 to 1985 Kresing was a
partner of G. Merckle in Münster, where he
has been running his own office since 1985.*

Lang Ladenbau GmbH

Rüdigerstraße 12
44319 Dortmund
Fon +49.231.92 10 40-0
Fax +49.231.92 10 40-20
info@lang-ladenbau
www.lang-ladenbau.de

*Ralph Rüdiger Lang (b. 1953) received trai-
ning in technical crafts and business before becoming a self-taught architect. In
1991 he began his collaboration with Dr.
Ing. Yongjie Cai in his own offices in
Dortmund and became CEO of Lang
Ladenbau GmbH. His work focuses among
other things on building among existing
structures, exhibition architecture, stadi-
ums, the catering trade and representative
interior architecture.*

Lange & Partner GmbH

Eichenstraße 41
20255 Hamburg
Fon +49.40.49104-29
Fax +49.40.49104-24
brief@k-lange.de
www.k-lange.de

*Lange und Partner GmbH was founded by
K. P. Lange and partners in 1992. The
company focuses on planning for listed
buildings, an activity that entails striking a
compromise between economic imperati-
ves on the one hand and conservation
strictures on the other. As well as its large-
scale modification work the firm is also
involved at the conceptual design phase
of projects.*

**Dipl.-Ing. Thomas Lau
Architekt**

Bebelallee 149
22297 Hamburg
Fon +49.40.51400-10
Fax +49.40.51400-120
Architekt.Lau@t-online.de

*From his position on the staff of various
architecture practices between 1979 and
1996 Thomas Lau (b. 1955) was especially involved in the construction of single-
family and multi-family houses, offices
buildings and car retail outlets. Since 1990
he has been a member of the Hamburg
chamber of architects. In 1997 he opened
his own office and has focused largely –
and successfully - on the refurbishment of
listed buildings and the construction of
hotels.*

**Mahmoudieh Design
Mahmoudieh Concepts**

Meinekestraße 7
10719 Berlin
Fon +49.30.88 71 79-0
Fax +49.30.88 71 79-16
info@mahmoudieh.de
www.mahmoudieh.de

Architect and interior designer Yasmine Mahmoudieh-Kraetz established her first studio in Los Angeles in 1986. Two offices in Hamburg and Berlin followed in 1992, with further branches in Barcelona and London opening in the late 1990s. Today, mahmoudiehconcepts and mahmoudieh-design draw up complete design and usage concepts for hotels, restaurants, shopping centres, offices and multi-use properties.

3meta märklstetter+fischer

Thalkirchnerstraße 82
80337 München
Fon +49.89.53 86 44 4
Fax +49.89.67 97 37 58
maerklstetter@3meta.de
www.3meta.de

Following her studies Evi Märklstetter (b. 1973) worked as interior architect at Büro Kolb in Augsburg and afterwards at Hugo Boss AG in Metzingen. Since 2002 she has been self-employed in Munich. Armin Fischer (b. 1966), a trained joiner and retailer, founded the "Freiraum" planners' office in 1993. Their collaboration began in 2003 when they successfully bid for the interior design contract for the "25 hours Hamburg" Hotel.

Cornelia Markus-Diedenhofen

Bismarkstraße 95
72764 Reutlingen
Fon +49.7121.14 49 9-0
Fax +49.7121.14 49 9-20.
buero@markus-diedenhofen.de
www.markus-diedenhofen.de

Cornelia Markus Diedenhofen (b. 1955) has been a freelance interior architect since 1985. Her office in Reutlingen near Stuttgart designs interiors for hotels, golf clubhouses, catering projects, office buildings, administrative premises and private houses. The project presented here was undertaken jointly with Hans Schönig, Sabine Müller, Heidrun Reichle and Ute Schweimeier.un Reichle und Ute Schweimeier.

José Rafael Moneo Vallés

Cinca 5
E-Madrid 28002
Fon +34.915.64 22 57
Fax +34.915.63 52 17

José Rafael Moneo Vallés (b. 1937) taught at the Escuola Tecnica Superior de Arquitectura de Madrid from 1980 to 1984 and went on to direct the Architecture department at Harvard University. Since 1990 he has been back at his Madrid office overseeing the development of many projects, among others Atocha rail station and the Tate Gallery Bankside. In 1996 he received the Pritzker Prize.

**Nalbach + Nalbach
Johanne Nalbach | Gernot Nalbach**

Rheinstraße 45
12161 Berlin
Fon +49.30.859 08 30
Fax +49.30.851 12 10
buero@nalbach-architekten.de
www.nalbach-architekten.de

The Nalbach + Nalbach firm of architects was founded in 1975 by Adjunct Professor Johanne Nalbach and Professor Gernot Nalbach. This Berlin-based company with branches in Dortmund and Vienna is active in town planning, architecture and interior design. A large number of its completed projects came as a result of successful competition entries. Along with residential properties, hotels, shopping centres and office buildings, Nalbach + Nalbach also carries out planning for the interior design of hotels.

**Neumayer & Partner
Architektur Design
Innenarchitektur**

Braunstraße 6
81545 München
Fon +49.89.41 30 97-0
Fax +49.89.41 30 97-70
info@neumayer-partner.de
www.neumayer-partner.de

Founded in the '70s, Neumayer & Partner are an internationally ranked office fully equipped for the planning and realisation of complete construction projects. They specialise in the development and coordination of sophisticated design concepts such as hotel projects. In their dealings with clients the architects set store on combining individuality and aesthetics with cost awareness.

Andrée Putman

83, avenue Denfert-Rochereau
F-75014 Paris
Fon +33.1.55 42 88 55
archi@andreeputman.com
www.andreeputman.com

Andrée Putman won the Design Achievement Award in 1991 and the Grand Prix National de la Création Industrielle in 1995 and has been a major force in the interior design of international hotels. "Elegance for me is when people hardly notice the work that's been put in. I have designed museums where the brief was not to compete with the works of art. In a hotel the guest is the work of art."

**Robinson Conn Partnership
Design Consultants
Richard Morton**

Ridings House,
68 Alma Road,
Windsor, Berkshire. SL4 3EZ
Fon +44.1753.83 00 55
Fax +44.1753.85 09 13
enquiries@rcpdesign.co.uk

Founded in Windsor in 1979, Robinson Conn Partnership is a leading international interior design company with offices in Kuala Lumpur and Istanbul. Over a period of 30 years its designs have resulted in the construction of important international hotel complexes that reflect the company's deep knowledge of a wide variety of cultures, a knowledge gained from their wealth of experience abroad.

Harald Schreiber
Atelier Harald Schreiber

Schadekgasse 18
A-1060 Wien
Fon +43.1.587 54 99
Fax +43.1.587 54 99
atelier@harald-schreiber.com
www.harald-schreiber.com

Harald Schreiber (b. 1952) has taught at Vienna's University for Applied Arts since 1983. With his public-space art and his drawings he has exhibited his work on approximately 130 occasions since 1976 and won numerous prizes. As architect and designer he has planned and shaped residential buildings, pubs and hotels across Europe.

Regine Schwethelm
von Heyden.Koch.Innen.Architektur

Osterfeldstr. 6
22529 Hamburg
Fon +49.40.41 49 85 86
Fax +49.40.41 08 45 0
c.k.christianekoch@web.de

Sibylle von Heyden has worked since 1994 as freelance, self-employed interior architect in Hamburg. Her trademark is brightly coloured, three dimensional representations of buildings and rooms, which she designs, plans and realises. She also designs furniture, lamps and a range of decorative features. She has involved, and continues to collaborate, with architecture cooperatives on numerous projects.

Sibylle von Heyden
von Heyden.Koch.Innen.Architektur

Osterfeldstr. 6
22529 Hamburg
Fon +49.40.41 49 85 86
Fax +49.40.41 08 45 0
sibyllevonheyden@web.de

Regine Schwethelm began her interior design career furnishing private villas in Munich and at the Starnberger See. In 1991 she moved to Berlin where she was responsible for planning and realising the design of the THG managerial floors and all the TLG offices (29,000 m² in total). Following her return to Hamburg she had specialised in hotels and clinics until 2002.

Jo Stahr

Weißenburgerstr. 30
81667 München
Fon +49.89.28 82 81
Fax +49.89.28 37 93
jo.stahr@gmx.de

Jo Stahr has been working as an architect on a vast range of projects for 30 years. He gives priority to the urban development aspect of a project and retaining some say in the course a project takes. "If we finish discussing money, functionality, community, neighbourhood, domestic factors and PR etc, and get around to talking about architecture, then I'll tackle those issues too."

Robert A. M. Stern Architects

460 West 24th Street
U.S.A. New York 10001
Fon +1.212.967 51 00
Fax +1.212.967 55 88
info@ramsa.com
www.ramsa.com

Robert A. M. Stern, architect, teacher and author, founded his office 34 years ago. It now has 140 architects, landscape architects and interior designers involved in the construction of housing, offices and administrative buildings. The company is active in 20 countries including Holland, Germany, Japan and Brazil, with Robert A. M. Stern personally supervising the design of every project.

Jan Störmer Architekten GbR
J. Störmer und H. Jaedicke

Michaelisbrücke 1
20459 Hamburg
Fon +49.40.36 97 37-0
Fax +49.40.36 97 37-37
info@stoermer-architekten.de
www.stoermer-architekten.de

Jan Störmer (b. 1942) founded the me di um group of architects in 1972. In 1990 offices were opened in London and Hamburg under the name Alsop & Störmer Architects, recording project successes such as the State Archive in Hamburg and Peckham Library in London. Since 2001 the Hamburg office has been called "Jan Störmer Architekten", and has gained some renown through its involvement with Hamburg's warehouse complex and the high-rise buildings at the Berliner Tor in Hamburg.

Architekturbüro
Dipl.-Ing. Helge Sypereck

Lyckallee 8
14055 Berlin
Fon +49.30.300965-0
Fax +49.30.300965-10
sypereck@gmx.de

The architect's office was set up in 1978. In addition to urban architecture projects and residential and administrative buildings the architects have seen to fruition large-scale exhibition and museum projects including the Gloria Gallery in Berlin-Chalottenburg (1987), the Herlitz AG offices in Berlin-Tegel (1988), the Falkenhöh garden complex near Berlin (1991-1997) and the master plan for the museums in Berlin-Dahlem (1991-2000).

nps tchoban voss Architekten BDA
A.M. Prasch P. Sigl S. Tchoban E. Voss

Rosenthaler Straße 40/41
10178 Berlin
T +49.30.283920-0
F +49.30.283920-200
mail@nps-tchoban-voss-b.de
www.nps-tchoban-voss.de

Founded in Hamburg more than thirty years ago, this firm has expanded its horizons with the opening of branches in Dresden in 1991 and Berlin in 1992. Sergei Tchoban, born in St. Petersburg in 1962, is the partner in charge of the Berlin office. The spectrum of the firm's activities covers office and business premises, apartments, hotels, cinemas, buildings for culture, trade and industry, town planning as well as working with heritage-listed, historical buildings.